SCIENCE
BUDDIES.

# 30-MINUTE RAINY DAY PROJECTS

Loren Bailey

Lerner Publications ◆ Minneapolis

Official Licensed Product
Lerner Publications Company
A division of Lerner Publishing Group, Inc.
241 First Avenue North
Minneapolis, MN 55401 USA

For reading levels and more information, look up this title at www.lernerbooks.com.

Main body text set in Hoosker Don't.
Typeface provided by The Chank Company.


**Library of Congress Cataloging-in-Publication Data**

Names: Bailey, Loren, author.
Title: 30-minute rainy day projects / Loren Bailey.
Other titles: Thirty minute rainy day projects
Description: Minneapolis : Lerner Publications, 2019. | Series: 30-minute makers | Includes bibliographical references and index. | Audience: Ages 7–11. | Audience: Grades 4 to 6.
Identifiers: LCCN 2018021506 (print) | LCCN 2018024711 (ebook) | ISBN 9781541542914 (eb pdf) | ISBN 9781541538924 (lb : alk. paper)
Subjects: LCSH: Handicraft—Juvenile literature. | Science projects—Juvenile literature.
Classification: LCC TT160 (ebook) | LCC TT160 .B314 2019 (print) | DDC 745.5—dc23

LC record available at https://lccn.loc.gov/2018021506

Manufactured in the United States of America
1-45075-35902-10/11/2018

# CONTENTS

For even more
rainy day projects,
scan this QR code!

# LET'S GET MAKING!

Stuck inside on a rainy day? No problem! There are lots of fun science projects you can complete in thirty minutes or less.

Whether you are in your classroom, your home, or your library, science is all around you. Get creative indoors and start experimenting!

After you've finished a project, add your own spin with something different. Just because you're inside doesn't mean you can't think outside the box! What will you make next?

# BEFORE YOU GET STARTED

Safety first! Some projects require sharp tools or hot objects. Ask an adult's permission before using them. Find a well-lit workspace. For easy cleanup, lay down some newspaper or cardboard.

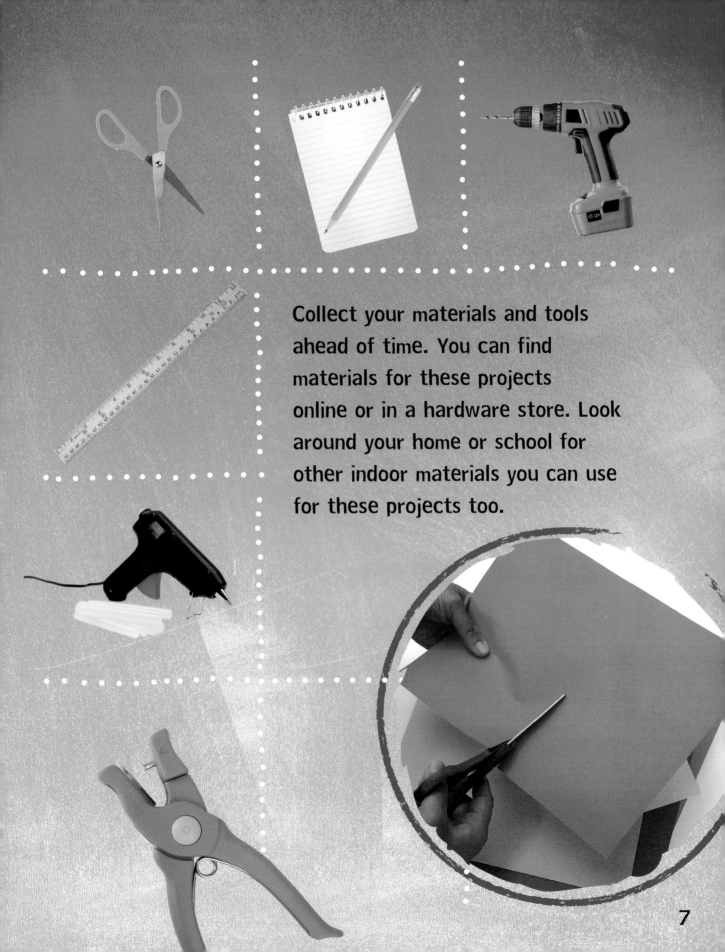

Collect your materials and tools ahead of time. You can find materials for these projects online or in a hardware store. Look around your home or school for other indoor materials you can use for these projects too.

# CAESAR CIPHER

Have you ever wanted to send a secret message to a friend? Create a code, or cipher, that only you and your friend will know! The Caesar cipher, named after the Roman emperor Julius Caesar, is a simple type of cipher where you replace each letter of the alphabet with another.

 **TIMEFRAME:**
**10 minutes**

**MATERIALS**

⇨ pen or pencil

⇨ notebook

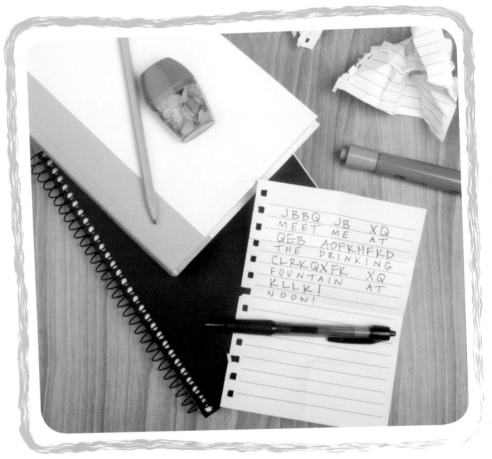

# SCIENCE TAKEAWAY

Cryptography is the study of writing or solving secret codes that are used for secure communication. Many of the earliest ciphers were easy to create by hand. These days, cryptography is used in computer science for keeping everything from emails to bank account information secure.

1. Write down the alphabet from A to Z.

2. Pick a number from 1 to 25. (If you use 26, you will just wind up with the original alphabet.) This number is your key. If you chose 3, you will shift your alphabet forward 3 spaces, and the last 3 letters of the alphabet will come to the beginning.

3. Shift the entire alphabet by the number you picked, and write it down below your original alphabet.

4. Explain the concept of a Caesar cipher to a friend.

5. Pick a message to write to your friend. Write down your encoded message using your shifted alphabet.

6. When you give your friend the encoded message, tell your friend the key, but do not write it in your message.

# BUZZING KAZOO

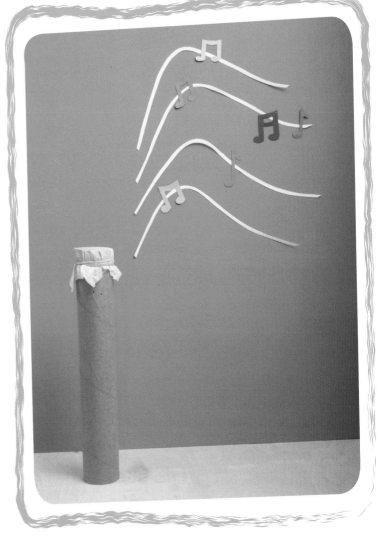

Bzzz-bzzz-bzzz! Kazoos are fun buzzing instruments. They turn any ordinary day into a musical one! Create your own kazoo, and make some music!

**TIMEFRAME:**
**10 minutes**

## MATERIALS

⇨ scissors

⇨ ruler

⇨ plastic grocery bag

⇨ paper towel roll tube

⇨ rubber band

⇨ sharpened pencil

## SCIENCE TAKEAWAY

When you speak, sing, or hum into the paper towel roll tube, the plastic vibrates. This vibration pushes the air and creates sound waves your ears can hear.

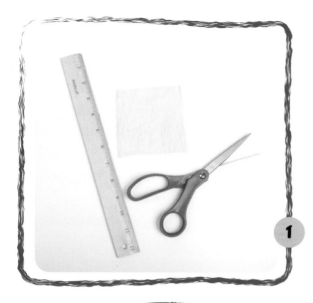

1   Cut a 4-by-4-inch (10 by 10 cm) square from the plastic grocery bag.

2   Place the square over an end of the paper towel roll tube. Use the rubber band to secure it firmly in place.

3   With an adult's help, use the sharpened pencil to poke a hole on one side of the cardboard tube, about halfway between the ends.

4   Put the uncovered end of the tube to your mouth, and make a sound. It should sound like the buzzing of a kazoo. You're ready to make a song!

11

# THAUMATROPE

Imagine a time with no television, no movies, and no cartoons. Believe it or not, those times weren't so long ago! What did those kids do when they couldn't watch movies? One of the most popular toys during that time was a great-grandfather of the modern cartoon. This toy was called a thaumatrope.

 **TIMEFRAME:**
**15 minutes**

## MATERIALS

⇨ scissors

⇨ white construction paper

⇨ ruler

⇨ pencil

⇨ marker

⇨ clear tape

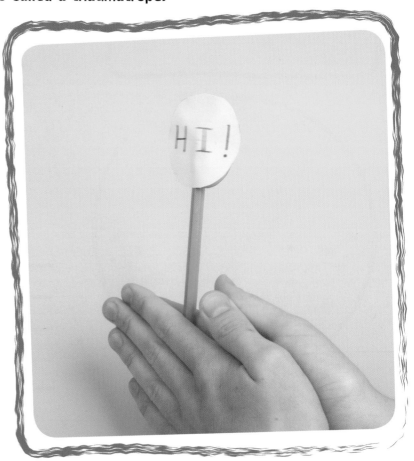

# SCIENCE TAKEAWAY

When you rotated the pencil between your hands, the letters on the two circles should have combined, so that you saw "HI!" appear. Even though the letters are on different sides of the circles, when you spin them quickly, your brain connects the images to appear as a word!

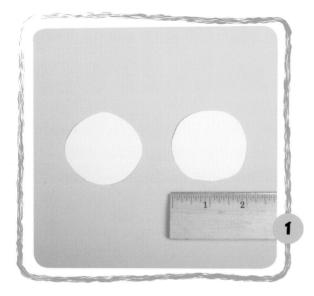

1. Cut out 2 circles from your paper, each about 2 inches (5 cm) in diameter.

2. Find the center of the first circle with your ruler. Lightly draw a line across the center.

3. Line up your ruler along the centerline. Then measure 0.25 inches (0.63 cm) from each edge of the circle. Mark the 2 points.

4. On the left side of the first circle, start at the 0.25-inch (0.63 cm) mark and write the letter **H** with a marker.

5. At the other 0.25-inch (0.63 cm) point, draw a large exclamation point with your marker.

6. Draw a centerline across the middle of the second circle. Line up your ruler along the centerline. Measure 1 inch (2.54 cm) from the right side, and mark that point with your pencil.

7. Use your marker to draw a large letter **I** at the 1-inch (2.54 cm) point on the second circle.

8. Place your pencil on the back of one of the circles, so the end is in the center of the circle. Tape it in place. Then line up the second circle with the first, and tape it to the other side of the pencil.

9. Hold the pencil between both hands, with the first circle facing you. Rub your hands together while looking at the circles. Rotate the pencil as fast as you can while still looking at the circles. What do you see?

# SUPER HEARING

Have you ever been puzzled by a faint noise nearby? Maybe you cupped your hand behind your ear, hoping to hear the sound better. What if you could make this cup huge? Create this gigantic hearing helper, and test what distances you can hear sounds from!

 **TIMEFRAME:**
**15 minutes**

## MATERIALS

⇨ 2 pieces of construction paper

⇨ clear tape

⇨ musical device with speakers

# SCIENCE TAKEAWAY

Our ears have pinnae—sort of like funnels for sound waves. Bigger funnels collect more sound waves, so you hear the sound better. Because they are big, however, they can also prevent a sound from reaching your ear canal. That's why they made the sound seem fainter when they were not pointing directly at the sound source.

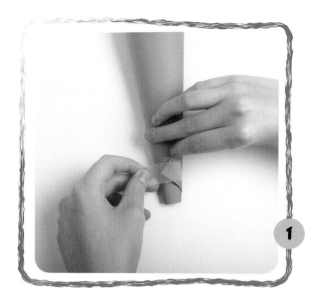

1. Roll a piece of construction paper into a wide cone. One side should have a hole small enough so it can rest in your outer ear, near the ear canal. (To avoid injury, do not insert anything inside your ear canal.) Use tape to secure the cone shape. Build another cone the same way.

2. Put your musical device on a low volume, so you barely can hear the sound. If you use a headset, put the volume on high so you can hear a faint sound without wearing it. Stand close to the speaker or headset, with an ear turned toward it. Listen to the sound. How much can you hear?

3. Place the cones in your ears so the small holes rest in the outer ear, close to the ear canal. Point the wide-open end of a cone toward the speaker or headset. Point the other cone in the opposite direction (away from the speaker or headset). Your head should be as close to the speaker or headset as it was before. Listen to the sound. How much can you hear this time?

4. If the sound is louder, turn the volume down until you can just barely hear it. Remove the cones and listen again. Can you hear the sound from the same distance without the cones?

5. Put the cones back on so the small holes are pointing toward your ear canal and one of the wide openings points toward the speaker. Turn your head so you are looking at the speaker and the cones are pointing to the sides. How does it sound this time?

# ALUMINUM FOIL SHIP

Have you ever wondered how a ship made of steel can float? And better yet, how can a steel ship carry a heavy load without sinking? It has to do with the density of the ship (including its cargo) and the density of water.

🕐 **TIMEFRAME:**
**20 minutes**

## MATERIALS

⇨ scissors

⇨ aluminum foil

⇨ clear tape (optional)

⇨ ruler

⇨ calculator

⇨ piece of paper or notebook

⇨ pencil

⇨ container such as a bucket, bathtub, sink, or dishpan

⇨ water

⇨ pennies

⇨ rag or paper towels

The density of water is 1 gram per cubic centimeter. To make your boat density calculations simpler, measure in centimeters.

# SCIENCE TAKEAWAY

Density determines whether an object floats or sinks. If an object is denser than the fluid it is in, the object will sink. If the object is less dense, then it will float. As you added pennies to the boat, its density increased and the boat floated lower until it finally became denser than the water and sank.

1. Cut a square of aluminum foil 30 cm by 30 cm and a square 15 cm by 15 cm.

2. Fold the aluminum foil squares into 2 rectangular boats, one large and one small. Make sure your boats don't have any leaks.

3. Calculate the volume of each boat. To do this, measure the length, width, and height of each and multiply these dimensions to get its total volume. Your boat's volume will be in cubic centimeters (cu. cm), or milliliters (mL). Write down each boat's volume.

4. Fill your container with some water. Place a boat in the water.

5. Gently add a penny at a time into the boat. To prevent the boat from tipping, try to balance the load as you add pennies. Keep adding pennies until the boat finally sinks.

6. Take out the sunken boat, and place it and the pennies on a rag or paper towels.

7. Count how many pennies the boat supported before sinking. Write this number down.

8. Repeat steps 5 through 7 with the other boat. Be sure to only add only dry pennies.

9. Multiply the number of pennies by 2.5 grams (the weight of a single penny) to determine how much mass each boat could support.

10. For each boat, divide the number of grams it could support by its volume in cubic centimeters. This is roughly the boat's maximum density before sinking.

# PAPER ROCKET

Blast off! Have you ever played with a model or toy rocket or seen a real rocket launch on TV? Make a simple rocket out of paper, and launch it by blowing into a drinking straw. How far will your rocket fly?

🕐 **TIMEFRAME: 20 minutes**

## MATERIALS

⇨ scissors

⇨ construction paper

⇨ pencil

⇨ clear tape

⇨ ruler

⇨ drinking straw

⇨ a clear space to launch your rocket, such as a large room or hallway

## SCIENCE TAKEAWAY

All flying objects need to stay pointed in one direction when they fly forward, without spinning or tumbling, which could cause them to crash. Rockets and missiles usually have triangular fins at their bases. These fins act like training wheels on a bike. They help prevent the object from tipping over.

1. Cut your paper into four rectangles by cutting it in half lengthwise and widthwise. Wrap one of the rectangles around a pencil to form a cylinder.

2. Tape the cylinder closed so it does not unravel (but do not tape it to the pencil).

3. Slide the cylinder off the pencil. Pinch an end of the cylinder shut, and seal it with tape. (This is the front end of your rocket.) Leave the other end open.

4. Cut out 2 right triangles (with a 90-degree angle in 1 corner) from another piece of paper. The long sides of the triangles should be about 3 inches (7.6 cm).

5. Draw a line that splits 1 triangle in half. Then draw 2 lines parallel to the first line (1 on each side), about 0.25 inches (0.63 cm) away from it.

6. Fold the triangle along these lines. The result should be 2 triangles sticking up in the air (the fins), with a flat part connecting them in between.

7. Tape the flat part to the side of your rocket, toward the open end (the base, or bottom, of your rocket).

8. Repeat steps 5 through 7 for the other triangle, and tape it to your cylinder on the opposite side of the first one.

9. With plenty of space in front of you—and no furniture or people—prepare to launch your rocket! Slide it over a drinking straw. Aim the straw forward, and then blow into it. Watch your rocket fly!

# CARDBOARD SCISSOR LIFT

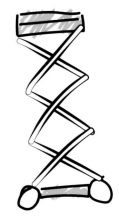

Have you ever wanted to reach something high on a shelf? Or have you ever watched construction workers who need to reach up a tall utility pole? A scissor lift can extend to a great length but also fold up very compactly. Build your own scissor lift from materials around your home or school!

🕐 **TIMEFRAME:**
**20 minutes**

## MATERIALS

⇨ corrugated cardboard (the thick cardboard with folds in between the smooth pieces)

⇨ pushpins or thumbtacks

⇨ hot glue

⇨ scissors

# SCIENCE TAKEAWAY

When you pushed down on the scissor lift ends, the lift got shorter and the Xs got wider. When you pulled the ends apart, the lift got taller and the Xs got skinnier. Some scissor lifts can extend to more than twice their original length.

1 Cut the corrugated cardboard into at least 6 equal-size strips.

2 With an adult's help, poke a pushpin through the center of 2 strips and join them to form an X.

3 Form an X with a pushpin and each remaining pair of cardboard strips.

4 Use hot glue to cover the points of the pushpins sticking through the back of the cardboard.

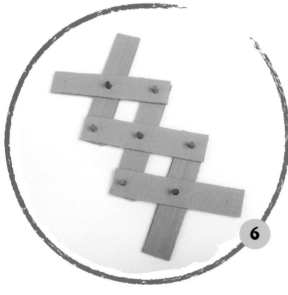

5 Use pushpins to join the top of an X to the bottom of another X. The pushpins should be in the same location on each strip.

6 Continue joining the top of one X to the bottom of the next X with pushpins. Make sure you alternate left to right which piece of cardboard is on top and which is on the bottom—this will keep your scissor lift flat when it is closed.

7 Repeat step 4 to cover the points of the pushpins added in steps 5 and 6.

8 Lay your entire scissor lift flat on a table or workspace. Hold the free ends of an X with your fingers. Try pulling them away from one another. Try pushing them toward one another. If you have more cardboard and pushpins, continue adding Xs. How long can you make your scissor lift?

# BE A COLOR DETECTIVE

Do you love to use bright and vibrant colored art supplies such as markers or paints? Do you ever wonder how these colors are made?

🕐 **TIMEFRAME:**
## 30 minutes

## MATERIALS

⇨ scissors

⇨ 2 white coffee filters

⇨ ruler

⇨ washable markers in brown, yellow, and any other colors you would like to test

⇨ 2 or more pencils (1 for each color you will be testing)

⇨ 2 or more tall drinking glasses (1 for each color)

⇨ water

⇨ 2 or more binder clips or clothespins

⇨ drying rack or at least 2 additional tall water glasses (1 for each color)

⇨ pencil

⇨ notebook

1. Cut the coffee filters into strips about 1 inch (2.5 cm) wide and at least 4 inches (10 cm) long. Cut at least 2 strips, 1 to test brown and 1 to test yellow. Cut an extra strip for each additional color you would like to test.

2. Draw a pencil line across the width of each paper strip, about 0.5 inches (1.3 cm) from the bottom end.

3. Using the brown marker, draw a short horizontal line on the middle section of the pencil line on one of the paper strips. Your marker line should not touch the sides of your strip.

4. Use a pencil to write the color of the marker you just used on the top end of the strip. (Do not use the colored marker or pen to write on the strips, as the color or ink will run during the test.)

5. Repeat steps 3 and 4 with the yellow marker and any other colors you would like to test.

**6** Hold a paper strip next to a glass (on the outside of it), lining up the top of the strip with the rim of the glass.

**7** Add water to the glass until the level just reaches the bottom end of the paper strip. Repeat with the other glass or glasses.

**8** Fasten the top of a strip to a pencil using a binder clip or clothespin.

**9** Hang the strip in a glass by letting the pencil rest on the rim. The bottom end of the strip should just touch the water level. If needed, add water to the glass until it is just touching the paper.

**10** Leave the first strip in its glass as you repeat steps 1 through 3 with the remaining strip or strips.

11 Watch as the water rises up the strips. When the water level reaches the top of each strip, remove the pencils from the glasses.

12 Hang your strips to dry in the empty glasses or on a drying rack. Note that some colors might keep running after you remove the strips from the water.

13 What happened to the color on the strips? Write down what you see. Can you identify which markers' inks used a mixture of color molecules and which used just one color molecule?

# SCIENCE TAKEAWAY

The variety of colors that appeared comes from colored molecules. The mixed colors separate from one another because some colored molecules are more attracted to the paper than they are to the water molecules. Marker companies combine a few color molecules to make a wide range of colors.

# DISK SIREN

Have you ever heard the loud wail of a fire truck siren? You might be surprised to know that the siren noise comes from blowing air and a spinning disk. Can you make sounds that way too?

🕐 **TIMEFRAME: 30 minutes**

## MATERIALS

⇨ drawing compass

⇨ pencil

⇨ card stock or cardboard

⇨ scissors

⇨ ruler

⇨ round hole puncher

⇨ double-sided foam tape

⇨ paper clip

⇨ high-power cordless electric screwdriver with a small hexagonal bit

⇨ drinking straw

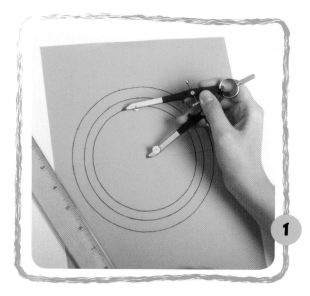

1 Use the compass to draw a circle with a 6.5-inch (16.5 cm) diameter on the card stock. Within the same circle, draw 2 smaller circles with 5.5-inch (14 cm) and 4.75-inch (12 cm) diameters.

2 Cut out the biggest circle.

3 Using the ruler and your pencil, draw 12 lines through the circle so you've divided it into 24 even wedges.

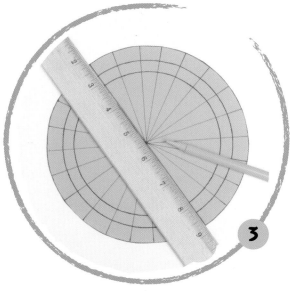

4 Punch a hole in the middle circle at every intersection of the lines and the circle.

5 On the innermost circle, punch holes at every other intersection of the lines and the circle.

6 You should now have a disk with 2 concentric rings of holes. The outermost ring has double the amount of holes compared with the innermost ring.

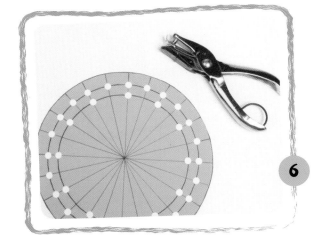

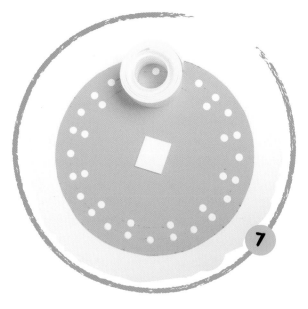

7  Cut a small piece of double-sided foam tape, and stick it on the center of one side of your disk.

8  Use the paper clip to make a small hole through the center of the circle and foam tape.

9  With an adult's help, put a small hexagonal bit in an electric screwdriver. Push the hexagonal bit through the small center hole of the disk so the foam tape faces toward the screwdriver. Use the foam tape to attach the card stock disk to the cordless screwdriver so it sits firmly on the screwdriver.

10  With an adult's help, hold the cordless electric screwdriver with the card stock disk attached. Run the cordless screwdriver on the highest setting.

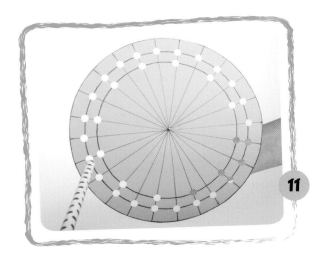

**11** Stand facing your adult helper. While the disk is spinning, place the straw closely in front of the outer ring of holes and blow hard through it. Be sure you do not let the straw touch the disk.

**12** While the disk is still spinning at the same speed, move your straw in line with the inner circle of holes and blow air through the straw against the disk.

**13** With an adult's help, play around with blowing at the rings of holes at different rotation speeds. Does the sound change with different rotation speeds?

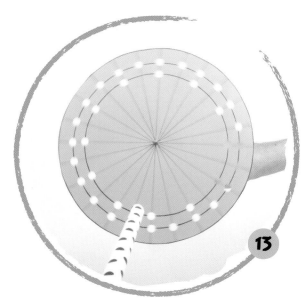

# SCIENCE TAKEAWAY

When you blew air against the disk, you created a sound wave. This sound wave comes from the air puffs switching between blowing through the holes and getting cut off by the card stock as the disk spins.

# WRAPPING UP

After you've completed your projects, make sure to clean up! Put away all materials, throw away garbage, and clean off your workspace. Store any projects you want to keep in a safe place so they won't get damaged.

A rainy day inside can be lots of fun! Think about what you learned while working on these projects. There's a lot you can do with materials you can find inside your home or school. The next time you're stuck inside on a rainy day, get creative!

For even more rainy day projects, scan this QR code!

# GLOSSARY

**cipher:** a code or secret way of writing

**concentric:** having a common center

**density:** the amount of something per unit volume, unit area, or unit length

**diameter:** a straight line passing through the center of an object or shape, such as a circle

**intersection:** the place or point where two or more items, such as lines or streets, cross

**molecule:** the smallest piece a material can be divided into without changing how it behaves

**parallel:** lying or moving in the same direction but always the same distance apart

**pinna:** the part of the ear that is outside the head and is made of cartilage. The plural is *pinnae.*

**sound wave:** a vibration that travels through air, water, or a solid object to reach our ears, resulting in a noise that we hear

**volume:** the amount of space an object takes up

# FURTHER INFORMATION

For more information and projects, visit **Science Buddies** at **https://www.sciencebuddies.org/**.

Challoner, Jack. *Maker Lab: 28 Super Cool Projects: Build, Invent, Create, Discover.* New York: DK, 2016.

Chatterton, Crystal. *Awesome Science Experiments for Kids: 100+ Fun STEAM Projects and Why They Work.* Emeryville, CA: Rockridge, 2018.

Mason, Paul. *25 Fun Things to Do on a Rainy Day.* Minneapolis: Hungry Tomato, 2019.

# INDEX

# PHOTO ACKNOWLEDGMENTS

The images in this book are used with the permission of: Design element (pencil) © primiaou/Shutterstock Images, pp. 1, 8, 9, 10, 12, 14, 16, 18, 20, 25, 29; © Visual Generation/Shutterstock Images, pp. 1 (clock), 30 (clock); © Mighty Media, Inc., pp. 1 (markers, drill, music notes), 7 (scissors, notepad, drill, ruler, hot glue gun, hole punch, red paper cutting), 8–29 (project photos), 10 (music notes), 11 (music notes), 12 (thaumatrope, teeter-totter), 14 (megaphone with music notes), 16 (boat), 20 (scissor lift), 22 (markers), 24 (markers), 26 (drill); © Tom and Kwikki/Shutterstock Images, pp. 1 (notebook), 9 (notebook); © Artur Balytskyi/Shutterstock Images, pp. 3 (rocket), 18 (rocket); © all_about_people/Shutterstock Images, p. 4 (boy with cup); © Sergey Nivens/Shutterstock Images, p. 5 (child with rocket); © GrashAlex/Shutterstock Images, p. 6 (girl with drill); © Tiwat K/Shutterstock Images, p. 31 (computer)

Front cover: © Artur Balytskyi/Shutterstock Images (rocket); © mhatzapa/Shutterstock Images (cloud); © primiaou/Shutterstock Images (lightbulb); © Sashatigar/Shutterstock Images (atom); © STILLFX/Shutterstock Images (background); © Visual Generation/Shutterstock Images (clock)

Back cover: © Artur Balytskyi/Shutterstock Images (gear); © primiaou/Shutterstock Images (pencil, magnet, square); © STILLFX/Shutterstock Images (background); © Tom and Kwikki/Shutterstock Images (beaker)